From Anglo-Saxon to *A*
North Gloucestershire in

by John S. Mc

I begin by thanking you for the privilege of being invited to give this year's Deerhurst Lecture, and by defining my terms. 'North Gloucestershire' I have interpreted as comprising the Domesday hundreds of Cheltenham, Deerhurst, Dudstone, Tewkesbury and Tibblestone, bounded on the north by the Warwickshire Avon, on the east by the mainly Cotswold hundreds of Greston and Wattlescomb, on the south by the hundreds of Bisley, Rapsgate and Whitstone, and on the west by the Forest hundred of Botloe (see Map 1). I have ignored the outlying parts of Worcestershire which were not incorporated into Gloucestershire until 1844 or 1931 (Alstone, Mitton, Teddington, Little Washbourne). I have, however, included Twyning north of the R. Avon, a detached outlier of Greston hundred. This is a compact and in the eleventh century an almost entirely rural area of 92,500 acres lying mainly within the Vale, one of the three regions considered by later geographers and topographers as making-up the modern (pre-1974) county of Gloucestershire, the other two being the Forest and the Cotswolds.

But the area also contained the county town of Gloucester and the very new borough of Tewkesbury, of which *DB* records (fol. 163c, *1*, 24) 'there are now 13 burgesses who pay 20 shillings a year; a market which the Queen [Matilda] set up there pays 11s 8d.'[1] The *DB* account of Gloucester (fol.162a, *G*, 1–4) focusses mainly on those urban houses held by magnates and the lords of rural manors, which probably functioned as 'town houses' when the lord was staying in Gloucester and as centres for selling produce from the rural manors and purchasing goods in the urban markets. In addition, this account informs us that there was a mint (which we know from its coins had been operating since late Anglo-Saxon times),[2] and a newly-built castle on the site of 16 houses 'which do not exist now',[3] and tells us that

> 'Before 1066 the City of Gloucester paid £36 at face value, 12 sesters of honey at that borough's measure, 36 dickers of iron, 100 drawn rods for nails for the king's ships, and certain other petty customary dues in the hall and the King's chamber. Now the City itself pays to the King £60 at 20 [pence] to the *ora*. The King has £20 from the mint.'

(The 'sester' was a measure equivalent to 2 lbs weight of honey; a 'dicker' was a unit of ten items; the *ora* was a Scandinavian accounting term normally of 16d, ten of which made the mark of 13s 4d, but which was often defined in royal accounts as 20d to avoid losses due to worn or clipped coins.) A fuller description of Gloucester is to be found at the beginning of

MAP 1. NORTH GLOUCESTERSHIRE HUNDREDS AND MANORS IN 1086

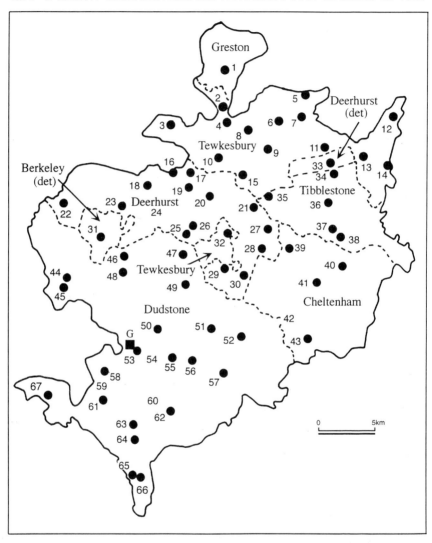

the 'satellite text' known to historians as 'Evesham K'. which has been updated to *c*.1100:

'Before 1066 300 burgesses in demesne in the city of Gloucester who paid £18 10s of rent a year. Of these 97 are residing in their own inherited property, and 97, French and English, are living in purchased residences which are worth £10, and they have held them for 12 years, that is £120. 24 out of these 300 lived within the

2

MAP 1.   North Gloucestershire Hundreds and Manors in 1086

TABLE OF REFERENCE

A. Arranged by Hundreds:

Berkeley (detached):
31   Ashleworth

Cheltenham:
42   Broadwell
41   Cheltenham
43   Leckhampton
40   Prestbury
48   Sandhurst
39   Swindon

Deerhurst:
17   Deerhurst
16   'Ellings'
27   Elmstone
25   Evington
21   Hardwicke
23   Hasfield
24   (Haw)
30   Hayden
26   Leigh
22   Oridge Street
18   Rye
29   Staverton
28   Uckington
20   Deerhurst Walton
19   Wightfield

Deerhurst (detached):
33   Woolstone

Dudstone:
52   Badgeworth
55   Barnwood
53   Abbots Barton
53   Kings Barton
46   Brawn
57   Brockworth
64   Brookethorpe
51   Churchdown
67   Elmore
63   Grove Court
66   Harescombe
49   Down Hatherley
16   Hempsted
54   Hide

Dudstone (Cont):
56   Hucclecote
60   Matson
44   Morwents End
45   Murrells End
59   Netheridge
47   Bishops Norton
50   Paygrove
48   Sandhurst
61   Tuffley
62   Upton St Leonards
63   Whaddon
50   Wotton
G   Gloucester

Greston (detached):
1   Twyning

Tewkesbury:
12   Alderton
5   Aston on Carrant
13   Dixton
35   Downing
9   Fiddington
3   Forthampton
12   'Hentage'
2   Mythe
6   Natton
11   Oxenton
7   Pamington
10   Southwick
14   Stanley Pontlarge
4   Tewkesbury
15   Tredington
8   Walton Cardiff

Tewkesbury (detached):
32   Boddington

Tibblestone:
36   Bishop's Cleeve
34   Gotherington
37   'Sapperton'
38   Southam
35   Stoke Orchard

MAP 1. Continued

B. Numerical Order:

1	Twyning	35	Downing, Stoke Orchard
2	Mythe	36	Bishop's Cleeve
3	Forthampton	37	'Sapperton'
4	Tewkesbury	38	Southam
5	Aston on Carrant	39	Swindon
6	Natton	40	Prestbury
7	Pamington	41	Cheltenham
8	Walton Cardiff	42	Broadwell
9	Fiddington	44	Morwents End
10	Southwick	46	Brawn
11	Oxenton	45	Murrells End
12	Alderton, 'Hentage'	47	Bishops Norton
13	Dixton	48	Sandhurst
14	Stanley Pontlarge	49	Down Hatherley
15	Tredington	50	Paygrove, Wotton
16	'Ellings'	51	Churchdown
17	Deerhurst	52	Badgeworth
19	Wightfield	53	Abbots Barton
20	Deerhurst Walton	53	Kings Barton
21	Hardwicke	54	Hide
22	Oridge Street	55	Barnwood
23	Hasfield	56	Hucclecote
24	(Haw)	57	Brockworth
25	Evington	58	Hempsted
26	Leigh	59	Netheridge
27	Elmstone	60	Matson
28	Uckington	61	Tuffley
29	Staverton	62	Upton St Leonards
30	Hayden	63	Grove Court, Whaddon
31	Ashleworth	64	Brookethorpe
32	Boddington	65	Haresfield
33	Woolstone	66	Harescombe
34	Gotherington	67	Elmore
G	Gloucester		

castle and 82 residences are waste ... The King has full jurisdiction over all these, and 10 churches are in the King's own jurisdiction. In Roger the Sheriff's time they paid £28 4s of revenue. Now they pay £46 ... The city has depreciated [in value] by £60.'[4]

The '10 churches' of *DB* can be identified as the two monasteries of St Peter's Abbey and St Oswald's Priory, together with the later parish churches of All Saints, St Aldate, St John, St Mary de Crypt, St Mary de Lode, St Michael, St Nicholas and St Owen, whilst 'the King's hall and chamber' represented the royal palace of Kingsholm which was certainly in existence by 1051.[5]

It is impossible fully to reconcile the information given in Evesham K with that given in *DB*, but, assuming that an urban burgess had on average five or six persons in his household, Gloucester had a population of between

1,500 and 1,800 before the Norman Conquest and, seemingly, between 1,000 and 1,150 in 1086, a loss of over one-third in 20 years. This apparent decline in population is difficult to accept when the amount rendered by Gloucester to the King rose from £36 in 1066 to £46 in 1086 (*DB*) and to £60 (Evesham K) *c*.1100, but the discrepancy is resolved if one includes the burgesses in Gloucester attached to various rural manors. Unfortunately estimates of this number vary widely: Darby accounted for 81 burgesses and 24 houses, a total of 105; another count put the number at 314 burgesses, a ludicrously high figure.[7] My own assessment of burgesses in Gloucester attached to rural manors is given in Table 1.

TABLE 1. Gloucester Burgesses attached to rural manors in 1086

| Reference | | | Number of | |
Folio	Chapter	Entry	Burgesses	Manor
162a	G	2	1	? Berkeley
162a	G	3	2? +	? Haresfield
162a	G	4	22	[Various unnamed]
163b	1	24	8	Tewkesbury
165a	3	5	4	Withington
165b	8	1	1 [?6]	Pucklechurch
165d	10	14	[?39]	? Abbot's Barton
166a	12	4	4	Broadwell
166b	20	1	30	Deerhurst
166c	24	1	1	Horsley
166c	28	1	11	Bisley
167d	39	2	3	Oxenhall
167d	39	6	2	Temple Guiting
168b	46	1	1	Great Rissington
168cv	50	3	5	Brimpsfield
168d	54	1	1	Frampton on Severn
169a	58	1	1	Bulley
169a	59	1	1	Lechlade
169a	60	1	7	Kempsford
170c	78	14	1	Woodchester

My total is 106 certain 'contributory' burgesses with, probably, another 45, depending on the interpretation to be placed on two *DB* entries: that for Pucklechurch mentions '1 burgess paying 5d' followed by '2 freedmen' and '3 Frenchmen there', so presumably these five men were also located in Gloucester; the entry at the end of the chapter for St Peter's Abbey, Gloucester, refers merely to unnumbered 'burgesses who pay 19s 5d.', so perhaps, at the rate of 5d or 6d per burgess implied by other entries, this suggests about 40 burgesses. At most therefore *DB* adds 151: this raises the total number of burgesses from 194 to 345 and the estimated population in 1086 or later to between 1,700 and 2,100.

The immediate results of the Norman Conquest may indeed have been damaging to Gloucester, with its render falling from £36 to £28 4s in 'Roger the Sheriff's time' in the 1070s (a drop of 22%), and this cannot in the main be attributed to the building of Gloucester Castle, whether the number of houses destroyed was 16 (as *DB* asserts) or 24 (as stated by Evesham K). Later, however, there had been an increase since 'Roger the Sheriff's time' of nearly two-thirds in revenue by 1086, perhaps linked to the immigration of both the new burgesses 'French and English, ... living in purchased residences' as well as the appropriation of 151 urban houses to various rural manors. Why '82 residences are waste' on the royal demesne is simply unknown, but the Normans may not necessarily be the culprits, for Welsh raiding remained endemic in the Anglo-Norman as in the Anglo-Saxon period.[8] At all events, the period from 1066 to 1086 saw a modest increase in Gloucester's population from between 1,500 and 1,800 to between 1,700 and 2,100, an increase of between 13% and 40%. By contrast, Winchcombe's population of about 300–350 (60 burgesses) remained stable between 1066 and 1086;[9] for comparison Tewkesbury's 13 burgesses, suggesting a total population of about 70–80 people, were indicative of its very recent origins as a borough under Queen Matilda, who died in 1083.

But, apart from Gloucester and Tewkesbury within our area, Winchcombe to the east, perhaps Cirencester where there was 'a new market' in 1086, possibly also founded by Queen Matilda (fol.162d, *1*, 7), Berkeley to the south where there was 'a market in which 17 men live' (fol.163a, *1*, 15), a borough fairly certainly in existence before 1066,[10] Thornbury, again a manor once Queen Matilda's with 'a market' (fol.163d, *1*, 47), and the ill-documented but clearly rapidly rising Bristol where *DB* simply records the existence of 'burgesses' (fol.163b, *1*, 21), urban life was still in its infancy in Gloucestershire. But there can be no doubt that Bristol was a rapidly expanding 'new town' in the eleventh century, with four moneyers at work under William the Conqueror and five under William Rufus; its population in 1086 was fairly certainly over 3,000 and perhaps over 4,000.[11] The great age of new boroughs and new towns, in Gloucestershire as in the rest of medieval England, was in fact to be in the two centuries between the reigns of Henry I (1100–35) and Edward I (1272–1307).[12] In the main, we shall be concerned with the doings of countrymen, of 'Hodge and his masters' as the Wiltshire journalist Richard Jefferies put it so expressively in the nineteenth century. But it is worthwhile pointing-out the connections between town and country already existing by 1086: the list of 'contributory burgesses' in Table 1 enables us to produce a partial picture of Gloucester's 'market region' in the later eleventh century (Map 2), and a similar map has been produced for Winchcombe in 1086.[13] A fuller picture of Gloucester's market region could be produced for later centuries by utilising the evidence of carrying-services recorded in custumals and extents and of purchases and sales in manorial accounts.

Since *DB* and the other products of the 'Domesday Survey', what contemporaries called 'the description of all England' (*descriptio totius Angliae*), are the main source-materials that I shall be using to reconstruct Anglo-Norman North Gloucestershire, I propose to begin with a summary of the

MAP 2. GLOUCESTER'S MARKET AREA IN 1086

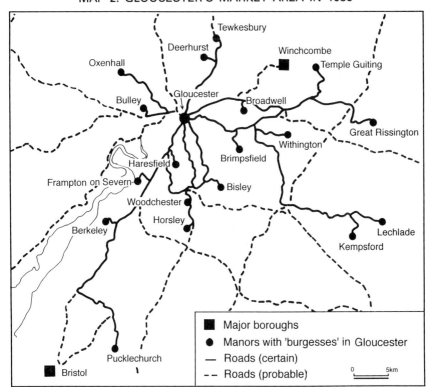

state of knowledge on the questions how and why the survey was made, and how reliable its information is likely to be. *DB* is in fact a misnomer, for there were in fact two volumes: 'Great Domesday' or 'Exchequer Domesday' or 'Domesday Book, vol.I' covers most of England south of the Tees and Ribble, apart from Norfolk, Suffolk and Essex which are contained within 'Little Domesday' or 'East Anglian Domesday' or 'Domesday Book, vol.II'. (Just to complicate matters further, 'Domesday Book, vol.I' has in its most recent rebinding in 1986–7 been divided into two halves to facilitate its preservation.)

We do know from the *Anglo-Saxon Chronicle* that the 'Domesday Survey' was initiated at a meeting of the royal council held at Gloucester which is commonly but wrongly dated to Christmas 1085. It was actually held in January 1086:

> '1085 ... Then at Christmas the King was at Gloucester with his Council, and held his court there for five days, and then the Archbishop and clergy had a synod for three days ... After this, the King had much thought and deep discussion with his Council about this country – how it was occupied and with what sort of people.

Then he sent his men all over England into every shire and had them find out how many hundred hides there were in the shire, and what land and cattle the King himself had in the country and what dues he ought to have each year from the shire. Also he had a record made of how much land his archbishops, his bishops, abbots and earls had and, though I tell it at too great length, what and how everybody who had land in England had in land and cattle and how much money it was worth. So narrowly did he have it investigated that there was not a single hide or yardland, nor indeed (it is a shame to tell but it seemed no shame to him to do it) an ox nor a cow nor a pig was left out and not entered in his record. And all these records were brought to him afterwards.'[14]

(Even counting from Christmas Eve, a court for five days followed by a synod for three days means that the Council could not have met before January 1st.) We also know that the 'survey', that is the basic collection of data, was completed in 1086: 'Little Domesday' finishes with the colophon (end-note),

'In the year 1086 ... and in the twentieth year of King William this survey was made not only for these three counties [Norfolk, Suffolk and Essex] but for all the others.'[15]

This conclusion is reinforced by the statement in an anonymous annalist writing at Worcester that

'All the writings of these things were brought back to the King. And the King ordered that all should be written in one volume, and that volume should be placed in his Treasury at Winchester and kept there.'[16]

Since we know that King William left England for the last time sometime after early August 1086, probably in August or September before autumn storms made a Channel crossing more dangerous,[17] and since it is highly improbable that the 'original returns' (as historians have called them) would have been sent overseas because of the risk of loss or damage, it is likely that the main survey was completed by about September 1086. Indeed, we now know that a significant stage must have been reached by June 1086, since, again according to the *Anglo-Saxon Chronicle*, 'all the landholders who were of any account all over England, whomsoever's men they were' were summoned to be at Salisbury on 1 August 1086 where

'they submitted to him and became his vassals, and
swore oaths of allegiance to him that they would be
loyal to him against all other men'.[18]

[What would later be called oaths of liege homage]. The summoning of 'all the landholders who were of any account all over England' could hardly have taken place unless at least preliminary versions of the lists of landholders to be found at the beginning of each county section of *DB* already existed. But since the Chronicle explicitly includes in its account of the 'Oath of Salisbury' both tenants-in-chief (those holding land directly from the King) and their vassals, those 'of any account all over England, whomsoever's men they were', it follows that summarizing the results of the inquest had already progressed sufficiently far for a list of manorial lords holding their lands from tenants-in-chief to be compiled in time for the sub-tenants as well as the tenants-in-chief to be summoned to be at Salisbury by 1 August. In order for that to happen, the summonses needed to go out from Winchester, still the capital of Anglo-Norman as of late Anglo-Saxon England, four to six weeks earlier, i.e. by mid-June. In short, the Domesday Survey was being conducted, and *DB* compiled, under considerable pressure of time, working to a final deadline which was perhaps Michaelmas or Christmas of 1087.

How was all this achieved? Two other contemporary or near-contemporary accounts provide clues. The first was by Robert Losinga, bishop of Hereford from 1079 to 1095:

> 'In the twentieth year of his reign by order of William, King of the English, a survey of all England was made, that is to say, of the lands of the several provinces of England, and of the possessions of each and every baron. This was done in respect of ploughlands and houses, and of men both bond and free, both those who lived in cottages and those who had their houses and their share in the fields, and in respect of ploughteams and horses and other animals, and in respect of the services and payments due from everyone throughout the land. Other investigators followed the first, and men were sent into provinces which they did not know, and where they themselves were unknown, in order to have the opportunity of checking the first survey ... And the land was troubled with much violence arising from the collection of royal taxes.'[19]

The second account was in the *Chronicon ex Chronicis* written by John of Worcester (formerly attributed to 'Florence of Worcester') in its final form *c*.1140, but drawing on earlier materials originally assembled after 1095 by 'Florence' (who died in 1118) and incorporating information from Eadmer *c*.1125:

> 'King William caused all England to be surveyed, how much each of his barons possessed, and how many enfeoffed knights, and how many ploughteams, villagers, animals and livestock each one possessed throughout the kingdom, from the greatest to the least, and what dues each estate was able to bear.'[20]

Another chronicler, Henry of Huntingdon, writing in the 1130s, noted that the king

> 'sent his justices through every shire ... and caused an enquiry to be made by sworn inquest how many hides (that is, yokes sufficient for one plough per annum) there were in every village and how many animals. He also had them enquire what each city, castle, village, farm, river, marsh and wood rendered per annum. All these things were written in charters and brought to the king, and they are preserved in the Treasury until today.'[21]

Finally, the *Course of the Exchequer*, written in the 1160s by Richard Fitz Nigel, the son of Henry I's Treasurer, recorded that King William 'after taking counsel sent his most skilful councillors in circuit throughout the kingdom.'[22]

From these sources, from detailed scrutiny of the changes in the terminology of *DB* in different counties, and from analysis of the so-called 'satellites' – copies of returns to earlier stages of the Inquest – it has proved possible to recontruct a reasonable picture of how the survey was made and how *DB* finally appeared.[23] It seems that the tenants-in-chief, having been briefed at the Council in January 1086, ordered their own stewards to make returns for their own estates, whilst sheriffs and royal reeves did the same for the royal estates. Such returns were probably initially submitted to county courts where they were checked against current and past returns to the royal land-tax or geld such as the surviving Devon, Dorset and Northamptonshire Geld Accounts and the Evesham K satellite, and were also seen by county juries, whose comments often are preserved in *DB*: of Westbury on Severn, for example (fol.163a, *1*, 11) 'The men of the county state, however, that the fir-wood [*or* Sapey] lay in Westbury in King Edward's revenue,' or, of Awre (fol.163a, *1*, 13), 'Outside the manor there are three members which were always and should be in it, as the men of the County testify.'

It is quite clear that the county jurors had full returns before them, 'laid on the table' as Parliamentary phraseology would later put it: how else would the abbot of Ely be able to reproduce, in the Ely Inquest (*I.E.*), full details of manors in 1086 of which the abbey had lost possession after 1066?[24] The importance of the jurors in county courts explains why the Cambridgeshire Inquest (*I.C.C.*) and the Ely Inquest preserved lists of jurors arranged by their hundreds, and why some satellites, notably the Cambridgeshire Inquest, are arranged by hundreds. County returns were then forwarded to the centres of regional 'circuits' where they were checked by the second set of commissioners mentioned by Robert of Losinga, and then summarized into draft circuit returns arranged by landholders under counties of which one survives, *Exon Domesday* for the south-western counties of Cornwall, Devon, Dorset, Somerset and Wiltshire. Fair copies were then sent, probably to the old Wessex capital at Winchester, to be summarized into the *Exchequer Domesday*; for reasons that are not clear, but perhaps relate to the crisis-conditions in 1088 after the death of William the Conqueror, the circuit-return for East Anglia was never summarized in the standard form of the *Exchequer Domesday* but remains in its present form as *Little Domesday*. (Dr David Roffe in a forthcoming monograph has suggested, however, that *Little Domesday* was in fact a first attempt at summarising the 'original returns', which was abandoned as too cumbersome before the *Exchequer DB* was compiled. Nevertheless, the fact that 'Little Domesday' was not replaced by a shorter version akin to the *Exchequer DB* but was hastily updated with the addition of some rubrication suggests that the final stages in the Domesday survey were abruptly aborted in 1088.)

Richard Fitz Nigel referred, as we have seen, to 'circuits', a term that had become much more familiar by his time because of their use by the itinerant justices of Henry I and the justices on eyre of his Angevin successors. But it is clear that England had been divided into seven 'provinces', as Bishop Robert of Losinga called them, returns from two of which were preserved in *Exon Domesday* for the south-western circuit (Circuit II) and in *Little*

Domesday for Circuit VII. The remaining circuits can be differentiated from each other by their use of certain formulas and terms which can be tabulated in Table 2 (on page 12) and mapped in Map 3:

MAP 3. DOMESDAY COUNTIES AND POSSIBLE CIRCUITS

It will be seen from this table that each circuit has a unique mixture of formulas and terminology, although relatively few are unique to one circuit. One important corollary of these differences between circuits in *DB* is that the central scribes, probably working under the direction of William of Saint-Calais, Bishop of Durham,[25] only had access to the final circuit returns such as *Exon DB* and had therefore no option but to copy the varying formulas found in each circuit return. Equally, this explains why the Domesday scribe frequently marked gaps in the text of *DB* with a marginal note 'r' or 'q' (for *require* or *quare*, 'find out', 'ask') where there were

TABLE 2. The Circuits of the Domesday Survey

	Circuit Number				
	I	III	IV	V	VI
Marginal M(anor), B(erewick), S(oke)		X			X
'It answers for x hides/sulungs'	X	X			
'Here x carucates'				X	X
1066 holder at start of manorial entries	X			X	X
1066 holder at end of manorial entries		X	X		
Land for x ploughs			X		X
Land or x ploughs and there could be more		X			
Land for x ploughs (many entries blank)	X			X	
Meadow: x acres	X		X	X	X
Meadow for x ploughs		X			
Wood: swine-totals			X		
Wood: swine-renders		X			
Wood: length and breadth			X	X	X
Wood: acres					X
Values: 1066, 1086			X	X	X
Values: 1066, later, 1086	X	X			
Female slaves			X	X	
Oxherds				X	

lacunae in the circuit return being abbreviated. In the event, the gaps were never filled-in, since work on *DB* came to an abrupt halt after 1088.[26] This variation in formulas and the unfilled gaps in the text are yet further indications of the pressure of time under which the survey was being conducted.

In the process of successive recopying and summarising, it is likely that some copying errors and omissions crept in, and certainly some information originally required was either never collected or was jettisoned at an early stage. The Ely Inquest preserves an early version of the 'terms of reference' for the Domesday Survey which ends, 'All this to be recorded thrice: as it was in 1066, when King William granted the manor, and now.'[27] Yet only for a few counties in Circuits I and III are values recorded 'when King William granted the manor', and the values are usually only recorded for 1066 and for 1086: generally the only data recorded for 1066 are the names of the landholders and the manorial values. Since there are some details of peasant populations in 1066 surviving even in the *Exchequer Domesday* – for example, *DB* (fol.162d, *1*, 1) records the number of tenants at Cheltenham in 1066 and then notes those 'added' by 'King William's reeve' – and *Little Domesday* generally records details of the peasantry in 1066, the details of 1066 peasants must originally have been collected and then generally omitted deliberately in the interests of brevity. On the other hand, although the *Anglo-Saxon Chronicle*, as we have seen, stresses the collection of details of livestock, it is obvious that the attempt to enumerate peasant livestock was soon abandoned if indeed it was ever implemented; *Exon DB* and *Little Domesday* only preserve details of demesne livestock, and even those were left out of the final version in the *Exchequer Domesday*. The 'making of Domesday' is summarized in Table 3 (on page 14).

Why was the Domesday Inquest made? This is a question to which no contemporary gives an explicit answer, and the modern historian can do no more than offer inspired guesses. It is perhaps significant that the account of the Domesday survey in the *Ango-Saxon Chronicle* is immediately preceded by a report of reactions to a threatened Danish invasion in 1085 by Cnut IV, a king with a claim to the English throne at least as good as that of William of Normandy (or for that matter Harold Godwineson!):

> 'When William .... found out about this, he went to England with a larger force of cavalry and infantry than had ever come to this country, so that people wondered how this country could maintain all that army. And the King had all that army dispersed over the country among his vassals, and they provisioned the army each in proportion to his land. And the people had much oppression that year ....'[28]

In the event, the Danes decided to murder Cnut IV rather than invade England, but the threatened invasion must have emphasized the king's lack of detailed knowledge of his kingdom.

The urgent need to billet and maintain a large force of foreign mercenaries – if the Chronicler is correct, larger than the 7,000 or so who had followed the Conqueror to Hastings – would have highlighted severe deficiencies in official information. How could the king have equitably distributed these mercenaries 'among his vassals', and how could the vassals in turn have 'provisioned the army each in proportion to his land' when the only information which was available to the king was the landholders' liability to the royal geld, according to assessments that were often decades if not centuries out of date? (The tenants-in-chief probably had better information on the holdings of their sub-tenants.) The king must therefore have realized the urgent need for an up-to-date survey of economic resources both of his own estates and of his barons' estates.

Equally, the title of many of the barons to their estates, in an age when nobilities increasingly wished to hold land securely and transmit it to their heirs, was shaky. It was not just that many titles ultimately derived from conquest, but that some lands had been acquired by dubious means from English or other Normans, without the king's permission in an age when it was increasingly accepted that all land was ultimately held from the king.[29] Hence it was desirable that where a royal writ or charter could be produced in evidence, it should be: the reduced geld-assessment of Lechlade after 1066 (fol.169a, *59*, 1) was verified by local jurors – 'All the County testifies to this' – and by Henry of Ferrers who 'showed the King's seal'. In only a few cases had land been acquired before 1086 by marriage or inheritance; the name of William Leofric, for example, shows he was half-English and he must be the son of Osgot who had held his manors, including Broadwell manor in Leckhampton, in 1066 (fol.167c, *38*, 1–5). Given this general insecurity and uncertainty, the emphasis of *DB* in nearly every entry on legal succession to named predecessors in 1066 is noteworthy, and it has

TABLE 3. The Stages of the Domesday Inquest

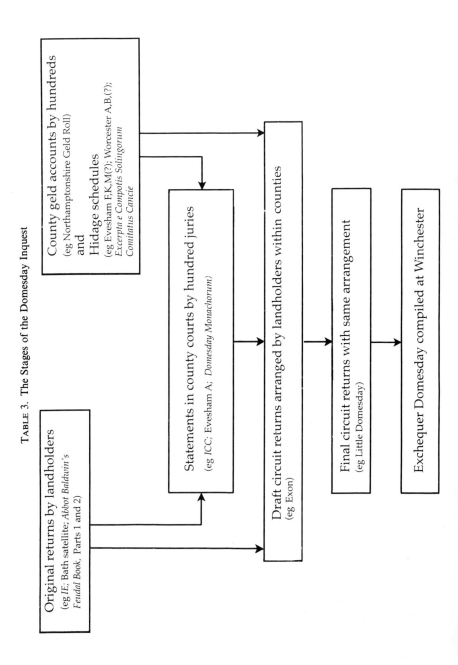

Original returns by landholders
(eg *IE*; Bath satellite; *Abbot Baldwin's Feudal Book*, Parts 1 and 2)

County geld accounts by hundreds
(eg Northamptonshire Geld Roll)
and
Hidage schedules
(eg Evesham F,K,M(?); Worcester A,B,(?); *Excerpta e Compotis Solingorum Comitatus Cancie*

Statements in county courts by hundred juries
(eg *ICC*; Evesham A; *Domesday Monachorum*)

Draft circuit returns arranged by landholders within counties
(eg Exon)

Final circuit returns with same arrangement
(eg Little Domesday)

Exchequer Domesday compiled at Winchester

been suggested with considerable plausibility that the Domesday Survey resulted from a bargain between the king and his barons at the Gloucester Council in January 1086; the king got the up-to-date information he needed on landholding and economic resources, and the barons in return acquired secure title to their lands.[30]

If, therefore, both king and barons had a joint interest in the reliability of *DB*, can we assume that the information it contains is accurate? For some earlier commentators, such as Canon Taylor writing on the Gloucestershire section of *DB* in 1889, this was an article of faith –

> 'I believe the text of ... Domesday to be almost faultless ... As Domesday Book was a work of man, there are also no doubt ... mistakes and omissions, but to acknowledge this is not to acknowledge that the man is living who can correct the master work' (*sic*!).[31]

– but we no longer live in an age of faith, certainly not of faith in infallible sources. Nevertheless, Canon Taylor's spirit lingers on in Australia, where G.D. Snooks believes in 'the comprehensive and reliable data-set presented in Domesday Book'.[32] How, then, are we to justify reliance on the text of *DB* as an historical source, especially when, as we have seen, the *Exchequer Domesday* is the end-product of a series of recopyings and summarisings at county, regional and national levels?

Internal checks can only really be applied to the geld-assessments, and omissions of whole manors detected, if two assumptions are valid, both of which are open to question. The first is that in 'Saxon' areas, such assessments are arranged to yield totals of multiples of five hides; the second that in 'Danish' areas such assessments are arranged to yield totals of multiples of six carucates. Although it seems likely that such assumptions are generally correct,[33] using them involves a strictly circular argument, and they should be applied with care. One Gloucestershire omission that can be detected using this method is at Marshfield, assessed at 14 hides (fol.163b, *1*, 20). All the surrounding manors, in Somerset and Wiltshire as well as Gloucestershire, have assessments in multiples of five hides, and the odd assessment of what became 'Great Marshfield' can be explained as resulting from the omission of the small manor of 'Little', 'Old' or 'West' Marshfield which can be traced in later records. Apart from the geld assessments, the only other, external, checks that can be applied to the data in *DB* are comparisons with the rare detailed estate-surveys of the Anglo-Norman period. No such surveys survive for N. Gloucestershire, but a comparison of the entries for the estates of the Abbey of Holy Trinity, Caen, in E. Gloucestershire in *DB* and in surveys of 1113–27 encourages belief in the accuracy of the data in *DB* (see Table 4 on page 16).

Overall, the comparison of the data in *DB* with that in the Caen Abbey estate-surveys a generation later strongly supports the accuracy of the *DB* data. For Avening the only major discrepancy is the disappearance of 30 slaves, but Avening had been a royal manor later given to the abbey, and the survey of Avening may be incomplete.[34] The data for Minchinhampton

TABLE 4. The Gloucestershire Estates of Caen Abbey, 1086/1113–27

	1086	1113–27
Avening:	24 villagers 5 small holders 5 mills 8 demesne ploughs 30 slaves	31 virgates 5 smallholders 4 mills and millers 8 demesne ploughs
Minchinhampton:	32 villagers 10 smallholders 8 mills 1 priest 5 demesne ploughs 10 slaves	$\left\{\begin{array}{l}\text{26 virgates} \\ \text{6 free men}\end{array}\right.$ 11 smallholders 7 mills and 1 waste 1 priest 5 demesne ploughs 2 swineherds, 7 millers
Pinbury:	3 hides 3 demesne ploughs 1 mill 1 smith 8 villagers 9 slaves	3 hides, 1 in demesne 3 demesne ploughs 1 mill 1 smith $\left\{\begin{array}{l}\text{1 church with a priest} \\ \text{7 villagers}\end{array}\right.$ $\left\{\begin{array}{l}\text{6 oxherds} \\ \text{4 cottagers}\end{array}\right.$ 3 female slaves

Source: 1086: *DB, Gloucs*, fol.163d, *1*, 49; fol. 166c, *23*, 1–2. 1113–27: M.M. Chibnall, ed, *Charters and Custumals of the Abbey of Holy Trinity, Caen* (Oxford, 1982), pp. 34–8.

in 1086 is close to that of 1113–27; one slave has obviously been enfranchised and has become a smallholder, and six of the villagers of 1086 have become free men three decades later. At Pinbury, nine slaves have become six oxherds and four cottagers and, interestingly, *DB*'s eight villagers are represented by seven villagers and a priest, the same assimilation of priests to villagers evidenced elsewhere in Domesday England, as we shall see shortly.

Another check that can be applied concerns the probability of copying-error, which, given the successive stages of summarising and recopying in the 'making of Domesday', would seem to be high: but a detailed study of the demographic data in *DB, Little Domesday*, and 'satellites' such as the Cambridgeshire and Ely Inquests for East Anglia and the East Midlands has revealed, against expectation, that the rate of detectable copying error is very low, of the order of 0.7%.[35] Even allowing for three stages of copying with accumulating copying-errors, a rate of 2%–2.5% is still as good as (if not better than) one can reasonably expect at any time in the medieval period.

DB does therefore in general terms seem to be a reliable source provided that we restrict our expectations to acceptable levels rather than absolute accuracy. Particularly with regard to statistics expressed in roman numerals, as all medieval figures are, error is easy and not easily detectable; 'xj' (11) can be miscopied as 'xvj' (16), 'xxj' (21), or 'xl' (40), or vice versa. We have already seen that the number of houses destroyed after 1066 to make way for Gloucester Castle is variously given as 16 in *DB* and as 24 in Evesham K; it is in any case more probable that the Evesham K figure is correct as being nearer to the original source, and this can be empirically confirmed by an addition of all the Gloucester figures for burgesses in Evesham K: $97 + 97 + 24 + 82 = 300$, the stated total in 1066. But there is no simple and obvious way in which an original 24 ('xxiiij') could be miscopied as 16 ('xvj') found in *DB*. At least three errors have been committed: 'xx' has been rendered as 'x'; 'iiij' has been (presumbly) miscopied as 'vij'; subsequently, 'vij' has been reduced to 'vj'. This is an object lesson against assuming that any individual statistic in *DB* is correct; nevertheless, we must not throw out the baby with the bath-water. With general copying-errors of the order of 1% per stage and a probable maximum of 3% overall, most *DB* statistics are likely to be accurate within reasonable limits and are perfectly usable so long as we can spot any glaring discrepancies.

What follows is an attempt to see what can be gained from a tabulation of the *DB* data for the rural manors in the hundreds of Cheltenham, Deerhurst, Dudstone, Tewkesbury and Tibblestone, together with Twyning, a detached outlier of Greston hundred. I have had to omit Ashleworth, a detached part of Berkeley hundred adjoining Deerhurst hundred, because its agricultural and demographic data cannot be separated from those for the other outliers of Berkeley in the south of the county (fol.163b, *1*, 15). For the same reason of amalgamated data, the details for the components of Deerhurst include the detached outliers of Calcot and Coln St Dennis twenty miles to the south-east, Kemerton north of the R. Avon, and Little Compton, Preston on Stour, Sutton under Brailes and Welford on Avon, 25 miles to the north-east and all in Warwickshire since 1844 or 1931. Nevertheless, the great bulk of the data in the Appendix refers to the core area of N. Gloucestershire as I have defined it.

How is the original information arranged? The account of each county, as Gloucestershire, is divided into numbered chapters for each major landholder, starting with the King, followed by his tenants-in-chief, archbishops, bishops and abbots, then earls and counts, then barons arranged roughly in alphabetical order of Christian name, ending with a miscellaneous chapter of minor landholders holding directly from the King ('Alfsi (OE Ælfsige) and other King's thegns' in Gloucestershire). Each of these chapters comprises entries for individual manors arranged within their constituent hundreds, which tell us if the manor was held in 1086 by the chief lord himself or had been granted ('subinfeudated' to use a horrid technical term) to a subtenant, usually but not invariably a knight; here or later in the entry the holder in 1066 is usually also named. The geld-assessment is given, with a note of any exemption or reduction accepted by the King, followed by the number of ploughteams on the lord's demesne, the number of slaves (where they existed, usually the men working these demesne ploughteams, often at the rate of 2 slaves per ploughteam). There or later other resources of the demesne are given, such as mills, fisheries, acres of meadow, woodland (in Gloucestershire measured in terms of average length and breadth), occasionally priests and churches, rarely a park.

But *DB* is not a reliable guide to the existence of either churches or priests: some 'satellites' indicate that priests were generally silently included within the ranks of the villagers – at Kennett in Cambridgeshire, for example, the Cambridgeshire Inquest mentions '6 villagers, 1 priest' which are represented by '7 villagers' in *DB*, an equivalence we have already seen at Pinbury – and churches were often 'appraised with the manors' as *Little Domesday* frequently notes. Thus the two undoubtedly pre-Conquest churches at Deerhurst, the priory and Odda's chapel, are not recorded in *DB*, fol.166b, *19*, 1, nor are many of the Anglo-Saxon churches so superbly studied by the late Harold and Joan Taylor or those which gave rise to village names such as Pucklechurch.[36] Archaeology and place-names are far better guides to the existence of churches in 1086. Numbers of the various groups of the peasantry then follow: free men, mostly 'riding men' in Gloucestershire, 'villagers' (a far better translation of *villani* than the misleadingly anachronistic 'villeins'), 'smallholders' (*bordarii*) and finally 'slaves' (*servi*, not to be translated as 'serfs' who did not exist in the eleventh century).[37] The total number of peasant ploughteams is then given, but as we shall see it is often clear that the chief holders of such plough-teams are the villagers; finally, the total value of the manor, or its customary rent, is given for 1086 and usually also for 1066.

The order in which the information is given in *DB* closely follows the order of the 'terms of reference' preserved in an early version in the Ely Inquest (*I.E.*):

> 'Here follows the inquiry concerning lands which the King's barons made according to the oaths of the sheriff of the county and of all the barons and their Frenchmen, and of the whole hundred – the priest, the reeve and six villagers from each village. They enquired what the manor was called; who held it in 1066; who holds it now; how many hides there are; how many ploughteams in demesne and how many belonging to the men; how many villagers; how many cottagers; how many slaves; how many freemen; how many sokemen; how much woodland; how much meadow; how much pasture; how many mills; how many fisheries; how much has been added to or taken away from the manor; what it was worth and what it is worth now ...'[38]

Virtually the only item not included in these 'terms of reference' were burgesses, but towns were clearly a late addition to the agenda of the Domesday survey; as in Gloucestershire, major boroughs were inserted at the beginning of each county section, before the list of landholders, and in Hampshire and Middlesex blank folios were left for the later addition of descriptions of Winchester and London which were never added. We have already seen that Bristol, certainly in the top six Anglo-Norman towns in terms of wealth and population, is represented by a bare mention of 'burgesses' in *DB*

How can we usefully summarize the information given in *DB*? Besides tabulating in the Appendix the 'raw' data on geld-assessment, demesne and tenant ploughteams, mills and other resources, the numbers of the various classes of peasantry, all for 1086, and the manorial values for 1066 and 1086, and also noting instances where we are exceptionally given population details for 1066, I have also tabulated some 'derived' data. First is the ratio of demesne ploughteams to all ploughteams in each manor, since this is the only guide in our period to the relative importance in the arable farming operations of the manor as a whole of the 'demesne', the lord's 'home farm' still often marked on modern maps as 'Court Farm' or 'Hall Farm'.

Second, an indication of the average size of peasant holding on each manor can be obtained by dividing the number of tenant plough-teams by the number of tenants (villagers only or villagers plus a quarter of the small-holders), a method pioneered by the late Reginald Lennard, and a translation of this ratio into practical terms of the usual medieval tenurial unit, the yardland, by assuming that one ploughteam usually cultivated the hide of four yardlands.

Third, an indication of total manorial population can be obtained by multiplying the total number of tenants, including male slaves who were usually married heads of household,[39] by 4.75, an average size of household first calculated by Peter Laslett and his colleagues for the early modern period,[40] but which I have since shown to be equally valid for the medieval period and for the Anglo-Norman era;[41] in these calculations, I have added 10 for the above average households of manorial lords where it is reasonable to assume they were resident on the manor, and I have rounded the final results to avoid any delusions of statistical precision.

For the same reason of avoiding misleading conclusions, the data in *DB* should always be studied *en masse*, for a reasonably large and coherent region, because it is fatally easy to construct a superficially attractive and plausible hypothesis from one or two entries which does not stand up when tested against a larger body of evidence. I am not for a moment suggesting that one cannot select examples to illustrate particular points, but one should be able to show that they are indeed typical of what one is trying to illustrate.

Let us start, as contemporaries would have started, with the holding of land, since this determined the distribution of wealth, of status and of power both before and after the Norman Conquest, since the basic structure of society, controlled by an aristocratic élite, did not alter. As George Orwell famously wrote in *1984*,

'Throughout recorded time, and probably since the end of the Neolithic Age, there have been three kinds of people in the world, the High, the Middle and the Low. They have been subdivided in many ways, they have borne countless different names, and their relative numbers, as well as their attitude to one another, have varied from age to age; but the essential structure of society has never altered. Even after enormous upheavals and seemingly irrevocable changes, the same pattern has always reasserted itself, just as a gyroscope will always return to equilibrium, however far it is pushed one way or the other.'[42]

Nevertheless, the personnel comprising the élite certainly did change dramatically. In 1066 there were no dominant landholders in North Gloucestershire, though several major magnates had estates in the region. King Edward the Confessor held Cheltenham, King's Barton and Matson; Archbishop Stigand of Canterbury held Churchdown, Hucclecote, Bishop's Norton and Swindon; Archbishop Ealdred of York held Brawn; Wulfstan, bishop of Worcester held Bishop's Cleeve and its attached sub-manors; the bishop of Hereford held Prestbury; the Deerhurst estate had been recently divided between the abbeys of Westminster and St Denis near Paris; Winchcombe Abbey held Twyning; the only major secular lord was Beorhtric son of Ælfgar who held Tewkesbury and many of its associated lands. But none of these men possessed major estates in our area; their main lands lay elsewhere, and some notable landholders in other parts of Gloucestershire, including King Harold (always 'Earl Harold' in *DB*), held no land here.

By 1086 there has been a dramatic change, the 'tenurial revolution' so-called by historians. Only four of the secular holders of 1066, or their descendants, still held land in 1086: Edward, lord of the small manor of Elmore, still held in 1086 but as a tenant of King William, as did Wiflet at Harescombe; Beorhtric, the lord of half Leckhampton in 1066, was a collaborator and in 1086 held the whole of Leckhampton manor, having been given the other half by King William; William Leofric, lord of Broadwell in Leckhampton, had succeeded to the lands of his father Osgot there and elsewhere in the county. Otherwise, there had apparently been a clean sweep of the Anglo-Saxon thegns. The lands of the archbishops, bishops and abbots of 1066 had mostly passed to their successors in office, but in the interim King William had become the major secular landholder in the locality, succeeding not only to King Edward's manors of Cheltenham, King's Barton and Matson but also acquiring Brawn from Archbishop Ealdred of York or his successor Archbishop Thomas and many manors in Dudstone hundred held in 1066 by individual thegns and by Alwine the sheriff, doubtless in order to consolidate control of the area around Gloucester where, as we have seen, he had erected a royal castle. In addition the King had also confiscated the Tewkesbury complex from Beorhtric son of Ælfgar; this, together with Beorhtric's other estates elsewhere in Gloucestershire and in several other counties, was held by Queen Matilda for her lifetime and then reverted to the King. Later mythology alleged that Beorhtric lost his lands because as a young man he had spurned Matilda as a wife, but there is no supporting evidence for this legend. Again, King William had consolidated his hold on the Tewkesbury area by dispossessing not only individual thegns and riding men but also Tewkesbury Abbey of some of its estates. The Crown had in twenty years become the largest single local landholder. Some great magnates certainly held manors in the region – William of Eu at Badgeworth, Hugh 'the Ass' at Brockworth – but their main areas of interest lay elsewhere.

From the holding of land, let us progress to the use the new Norman lords made of the land, although as we shall see, very few were residing on their manors in 1086. That, however, did not stop lords from running their estates efficiently either by means of their own stewards or by leasing the demesnes to a 'farmer', a method that minimised risk and was popular with lords in the eleventh and twelfth centuries.[43] Agriculture in the medieval period was predominantly arable-farming, which explains why the principal criterion used by *DB* to assess agriculture, both of the lords and of their peasants, is the number of working 'ploughs' (i.e. ploughteams, usually of eight oxen yoked in pairs). The number of demesne ploughs is the best guide we have to the size of the lord's demesne in each manor before the more detailed surveys and extents of the thirteenth and fourteenth centuries provide us with acreages. In N. Gloucestershire the demesne ploughs varied from one at Brawn, Elmore, Leckhampton, Stoke Orchard and Upton St Leonards to 13 at Hardwicke and its outliers and also at Tewkesbury and 15 at Woolstone and its outliers, but all these were 'complex', multi-focal manors, as were another collection of Deerhurst outliers with 11.5 ploughs, Abbot's Barton and its sub-manors with 9 ploughs, Haresfield and its sub-manors with 8 ploughs and Southam and its sub-manors, also with 8 ploughs. In all these entries the total number of ploughs is an amalgamation of those at several centres; the normal range was from two to six, and the overall average was just over 4 ploughs, perhaps equivalent to a demesne area of about 500 acres.

Even so, the number of demesne ploughs will tend to understate the size of the demesnes. The reason is that demesnes were not usually ploughed by the demesne ploughs alone; the tenants, certainly the villagers and small-holders, also provided what the thirteenth-century writers would call 'week-work', regular labour-services, including ploughing the lord's demesne with their own ploughs. Thus the Caen Abbey estate-survey for Pinbury refers to '7 villagers working 5 days a week, ... 4 cottagers working 3 days [a week]', whilst at Avening and Minchinhampton the surveys mention 'virgates rendering work (*ad opus*)'.[44] Sometimes, abnormally, even the free-men in Gloucestershire had to provide such labour-services: at Southwick and its associated outliers in 1066 '9 riding men ... ploughed and harrowed at the lord's court' (fol.163b, *1*, 24) and at Elmstone and its outliers of Deerhurst 'Riding men, that is, free men, held of this manor's land before 1066 who all, however, ploughed, harrowed, scythed and reaped for the lord's work' (fol.166b, *19*, 2). It is, therefore, clear that the imposition of labour-services on free men was not a Norman imposition in Gloucester-shire but predated the Conquest. Moreover, the Norman Conquest does not seem to have made much difference to the exploitation of manors by their lords. The total value of the manors in N. Gloucestershire for which *DB* provides figures in both 1066 and 1086 fell from £1406 10s to £1373 10s, a decrease of only 2.3%. Given the difficulties in comparing any two isolated years when we do not know if either was typical of the surrounding years –

and we may legitimately think that neither 1066 nor 1086 were 'normal' years – a change of the order of 2% is well within the margins of error. Certainly it does not justify any conclusion about long-term decline since 1066. In some manors, such as Cheltenham and Tewkesbury, we are explicitly told population has increased since 1066, and in some other manors values have also increased between 1066 and 1086 – Abbots Barton, Prestbury, Swindon, Uckington and its outliers, Wotton.

For the same reason – the existence of labour-services – the proportion of demesne ploughs in the total number of ploughs per manor will underrate the proportion of manorial land constituting the demesne. Nevertheless, the fertility of the Northern Vale and perhaps also the demand from Gloucester, both for its citizens and the garrison of the castle and also for resale in its markets, meant that demesnes occupied more of the local soil than elsewhere in Gloucestershire, averaging 42% and ranging from 12– 15% up to 100%. But despite the attractiveness of demesne- cultivation to local lords, this had not yet led in N. Gloucestershire to a 'depression of the peasantry' after the Conquest. If we adopt Reginald Lennard's method of dividing the number of tenants' ploughs by the number of tenants in order to obtain an average number of ploughs per tenant, this average is rarely less than half a plough and is frequently one plough or more per villager. Where it is possible to separate the ploughs held by different groups of tenants we can arrive at more precise and meaningful results. 'A priest and a riding man' at Prestbury had 2 ploughs; 2 freemen at King's Barton held 9 ploughs; 'a riding man' at Alderton held 1 plough and at Bishop's Cleeve a priest and a riding man each had two ploughs. In N. Gloucestershire at all events the free men, riding men and a minority of priests, formed a 'peasant aristocracy' with an average of more than two ploughs apiece, suggesting that in real terms they held more than two hides each, say about 300 acres. At the other end of the social scale, ploughs held only by smallholders (*bordarii*) are occasionally mentioned: at the main manor of Leckhampton 9 smallholders held 3 ploughs; at King's Barton the 8 smallholders added by the king's reeve had 1 plough; at Brawn 7 smallholders had 2 ploughs; at Upton St Leonards 4 smallholders had 2 ploughs. *In toto*, 28 smallholders had 8 ploughs, barely more than a quarter of a plough each, equivalent to a yardland of perhaps 30–40 acres. By contrast, the villagers' average number of ploughs represents an average holding of 3.5 yardlands overall, with many villagers in 1086 still having the full hide of 4 yardlands that had been regarded in Anglo-Saxon times as the normal 'land of one family', roughly 120–160 acres.

Obviously, such group averages conceal wide variations in the size of holding that are only apparent in *DB* in Middlesex where statistics of peasant holdings are frequently given and elsewhere in England in more detailed surveys of the twelfth, thirteenth and fourteenth centuries. The nearest local example I know is a previously unrecognised survey of 'churchscot' owing to Winchcombe Abbey of about 1140 embedded in the abbey's *Landboc*.

TABLE 5. Peasant landholding in the Winchcombe Area, *c.* 1140:

	Number of yardlands per peasant:			
	0.5	1	1.5	2
Number of peasants/Place				
Hawling:	0	8	2	7
'Rodes':	5	4	0	0
Winchcombe:	1	1	1	0
Greet:	3	8	0	2
Coates:	6	8	0	0
Gretton:	4	7	1	0
Stanley Pontlarge:	0	4	0	0
[?Sudeley:]	0	7	0	0
Totals:	19	47	4	9

This gives the names and holdings of individual peasants at Hawling, Sudeley and Winchcombe, summarized in Table 5:[45]

These figures from the Cotswolds are not of course directly comparable though they do show the extent to which averages concealed variation in peasant landholding. In 1086 at Hawling (fol.170b, *72*, 1) 20 villagers and 5 smallholders held 9 ploughs, so that the average villager's holding was about 1.5–2 yardlands. At Stanley Pontlarge (fol.163c, *1*, 33) there were 4 villagers with 2 ploughs in 1086, again implying an average villager's holding of 2 yardlands, but by *c.*1140 the lord, Roger Parvus, had annexed 6 yardlands 'once held by men of servile condition', so that direct comparison is not possible. Nor is comparison easy between the entries for Winchcombe and its tithings *c.*1140 because it is uncertain what *DB* manors were involved. However, the 'fee of Sudeley' mentioned as a heading in the survey comprised the manors of Sudeley and Toddington (fol.169b, *61*, 1–2); on these two manors there were in 1086 2 free men, 35 villagers and 15 smallholders with 21 ploughs, suggesting an average villager's holding of 2 yardlands. But population-growth and demesne-expansion, as at Stanley Pontlarge, prevents any certain conclusions being drawn.

Apart from the broad social groupings of 'free men' (mostly 'riding men' in Gloucestershire), 'villagers', 'smallholders' and 'slaves', *DB* is not a good source of information on local social structure in the countryside below the level of lay lords of manors who were mostly barons or knights. The recorded male population of rural N. Gloucestershire in 1086 is divided as follows:

TABLE 6. Male population of North Gloucestershire in 1086

	Free Men	Villagers	Smallholders	Slaves
Numbers	48	495	306	376
Percentage of total:	3.9	40.4	25.0	30.7

The free men were a tiny minority, and the slaves were already declining in numbers, as at Tewkesbury (fols.163b, c, *1*, 24) where 50 slaves, 'male and female', in 1066 had been reduced to 22 in 1086, and at Hailes where 'There were 12 slaves whom William [Leofric] freed' (fol.167c, *38*, 2). Slaves, indeed, had disappeared all over England before the death of Henry I, being enfranchised to join the smallholders: thus at Hailes in 1086 the former 12 slaves are represented by '11 smallholders'.[46] That the process of enfranchising slaves had started well before 1086 is proved by the presence in *DB* of 'freedmen' (*coliberti*) at the Tewkesbury outliers (fol.163b, *1*, 24), Fiddington (fol.163c, *1*, 31) and probably at Gloucester (fol.165b, *8*, 1) in our region and at Barton Regis (fol.163b, *1*, 21), Berkeley (fol.163a, *1*, 15), Dymock (fol.164a, *1*, 53), Hawkesbury (fol.166a, *14*, 2) and the outliers of Westbury on Trym (fol.164d, *3*, 1) elsewhere in the county. The tendency of freedmen to occur near the larger towns may indicate that market forces are tending to encourage the liberation of slaves because they are seen as an uneconomic and inefficient labour-force.[47]

Estimating total population for the region requires first considering two problems. The first is the 'multiplier' needed to convert data on males, who are generally agreed by historians to be married heads of household, into total population. This assumption that recorded males were heads of households can be justified by exceptional entries such as that for Hidcote Bartrim in N.E. Gloucesterhire (fol.166a, *12*, 9): 'The wives of 4 villagers lately dead have 1 plough.' The second problem is the allowance to be made for omissions. To summarize the current state of research on these matters, the Anglo-Norman household is now believed to be of the same size, on average 4.75 people, with the core family having the same 'nuclear' structure as later in English history.[48] The allowance to be made for omissions is thought not to be greater than 5%.[49] Yet it is clear that the households of the higher social groups are much larger than the average, since the biological family will be surrounded by servants, including in the medieval period household knights and other armed retainers. Therefore the estimated totals of manorial population, derived by multiplying the number of tenants by 4.75, should be increased to allow for the larger household of a resident lord. However, the squirearchy so familiar to later English history is absent in the aftermath of the Norman Conquest which had seen not only the disappearance of the Old English thegns but also a radical change in the structure of the ruling class; in round numbers, 4,000 Anglo-Saxon and Anglo-Danish thegns had been replaced by about 250 'Norman' barons and about the same number of knights holding larger estates. These mostly lived in castles at the centre of their 'honours' or 'baronies': in 1100 it has been estimated there were about 500 castles in existence, of which the largest, as at Gloucester, belonged to the King.[50]

The chief residences even of the knights who held land only or mainly in Gloucestershire were not necessarily in our area: Gerard the Chamberlain's main manor was at Kemerton (fol.163d, *1*, 41; fol.166b, *19*, 2), not at Aston on Carrant; John the Chamberlain's main manor was an outlier of Fairford at Eastleach Turville (fol.163d, *1*, 50), not Mythe in Twyning. In N. Gloucestershire Bernard held both a part of Fiddington and Stoke Orchard; the latter was his main manor. In short, only a few of the subtenants were resident lords: Avenel the cook at Netheridge in Quedgeley, Bernard at Stoke Orchard as we have just seen, Edward at Elmore, Ralph [of Cardiff] at Walton Cardiff named after his family, Wiflet (one of the survivors from before 1066) at Harescombe, William Breakwolf at Wotton, the two unnamed free men at Matson, perhaps Walkelin 'the bishop of Winchester's nephew' at Bishop's Norton. Humphrey of Maidenhill, lord of Upton St Leonards, took his name from Maidenhill in Sezincote (fol.170a, *70*, 1–2), but must have lived at Upton: Maidenhill had been depopulated since 1066 and was valued in 1086 'only for the meadows'. None of these resident lords were substantial land holders and adding 10 to the calculated manorial populations will be adequate allowance for their households. It is therefore possible to calculate total manorial populations, which have been deliberately 'rounded' to avoid any impression of statistical precision.

What it is rarely possible to do is to produce estimates of parish populations. The exceptions where this can be achieved, because it seems certain that the *DB* manor coincides in area with the later parish (sometimes including its chapelries, as at Churchdown) are listed in Table 7. Estimated parish

TABLE 7. Selected Parish populations in
North Gloucestershire in 1086

Badgeworth	240
Brockworth	100
Cheltenham	260
Churchdown	140
Bishop's Cleeve	210
Forthampton	120
Hucclecote	80
Leckhampton	140
Oxenton	90
Stanley Pontlarge	60
Upton St Leonards	40
Great Washbourne	80
Whaddon	90

populations range from 40 to 260, the average being 130. If these figures are typical of the whole area, most N. Gloucestershire villages in 1086 were small compared to their successors in later centuries. Yet we are fairly certain that the two centuries after 1086 saw English population at least doubling if not trebling, from something like 2,000,000 in 1086 to perhaps 5–6 millions about 1300.[51] Moreover, our conclusion about local population is subject to the caveat that much of our area, including King's Barton, the two groups of Deerhurst manors, Haresfield and the Tewkesbury manors, are large 'composite', multifocal manors in which population-data is recorded for amalgamated groups of sub- manorial units which often do not correspond with later parishes.

It is impossible, for example, to disaggregate the figures (apart from the hidages) for the individual tithings within Tewkesbury manor or the divided Deerhurst complex. The population of N. Gloucestershire can be estimated as about 6,000 in the country side and no more than about 2,000 in the two local boroughs of Gloucester and Tewkesbury, together 8,000 in town and country.

Whether the rural population had increased since 1066 is even less certain than whether the urban population had risen. The sole local data bearing on this point comprises the entries for Cheltenham, where the king's reeve had added 4 villagers and 2 smallholders since 1066, an increase of 16%, and King's Barton, where the king's reeve had added 8 smallholders since 1066, an increase of 24%. If the experience of these two manors was typical of the region as a whole, local population increased by roughly one-fifth in twenty years. But, since they were royal manors, Cheltenham and King's Barton may well not be typical; in any case, as I have already remarked, two manors are not a safe basis for generalization. The evidence from a third royal manor, Tewkesbury, is ambiguous: it is unclear whether the 22 slaves recorded later in this entry are in addition to, or in substitution for, the 50 slaves recorded in 1066.

At this point the limitations of *DB* as an historical source come into sharp focus, and I conclude by briefly outlining the additional, mainly later sources, which we need to use, with due caution, to produce a fuller picture of N. Gloucestershire in the years around 1086. Important though the Norman Conquest was, significant though the discontinuities were, there was also much continuity, above all in the landscape,[52] for which later sources are relevant and valid evidence. The evidence of place-names and field-names,[53] many recorded as late as the eighteenth and nineteenth centuries in enclosure maps, tithe maps and the early large-scale Ordnance survey maps,[54] or in title deeds[55] can throw much light on the local landscape. Early charters can illuminate the doings of lords and peasants from the twelfth century onwards, and these were often copied into monastic deed-registers or cartularies, notably, for our area, the Cirencester Abbey cartulary so splendidly edited by the late Charles Ross and the still unprinted series of cartularies for Llanthony Priory.[56] Later manorial surveys, from the 'extents' of the thirteenth century to the detailed maps with reference books of the seventeenth to nineteenth centuries, can inform us of such basic matters as the number of great 'open fields' per parish into which the cultivated area of most of medieval England was divided and communally cultivated before enclosure as well as giving acreages for demesnes and often also for tenants' holdings.[57]

Such surveys, as well as early charters, can also display the gradual replacement after 1066 of most Old English forenames by continental names such as Robert and William and biblical names such as John and Thomas, as Cecily Clark was the first to show,[58] an aspect of the assimilation of, and acceptance of, the Normans by the English so splendidly chronicled by Ann Williams, a previous Deerhurst lecturer.[59] A preliminary analysis of the peasants' names in the Winchcombe 'churchscot' surveys shows that by c.1140 two-thirds had adopted continental or biblical forenames. This helps to explain why, proverbially, Englishmen are now called 'Tom, Dick and Harry', none of which is Old English! Finally, there is the physical evidence of the surviving landscape and the buildings on it, the 'environment' to use a trendy phrase. The open fields which I have just mentioned have often left recognisable traces in the form of long narrow fields or the characteristically corrugated surface of 'ridge-and- furrow' on the land. And why, in village after village, is the manor-house to be found next to the parish church? The reason goes back to the period from roughly 1000 to 1300, when old large minster-parishes served by groups of canons or monks, such as Deerhurst or Tewkesbury, were being divided into smaller parishes served by individual parish priests.[60] In the main, these new parish churches were built by manorial lords, who appointed the priest (often their own younger sons!) and did not see why they should walk further than they needed to on a wet Sunday. So the parish church, 'his church' as the lord saw it, was built next to the manor-house, even attached to the manor-house as in the case of Odda's chapel at Deerhurst. This sort of evidence will naturally be far more familiar to you than to an outsider such as myself, yet it is important that it should be studied and recorded because it is often more perishable, more liable to destruction or unrecorded change, than documents now safely stored in the Public Record Office at Kew, the British Library in Euston Road or the Gloucestershire Record Office in Alvin Street, Gloucester. In the final analysis, local history can only be successfully written if it unites the expertise of the academic professional with the knowledge of the interested local inhabitant.[61]

NOTES

1. References to Domesday Book (*DB*) are to the Phillimore edition under the general editorship of John Morris. This is the only readily available version which permits precise reference to individual entries, the folio number being followed by the column number (a–b on the recto, c–d on the verso), the chapter number, in italics, and the entry number. A facsimile edition for Gloucestershire, edited by Ann Williams, was published in London in 1989.

2. R. H. M. Dolley, *The Norman Conquest and the English Coinage* (London, 1966), p. 14; E. J. Harris, 'The Moneyers of the Norman Kings and the types they are known to have struck, Part 8' (*Seaby Coin and Medal Bulletin*, no.794 (1984), pp. 246–7); *Victoria County History of Gloucestershire*, vol. IV (1988), pp. 8, 12–13, 64.

3. H. Hurst, 'The Archaeology of Gloucester Castle' (*Transactions of the Bristol and Gloucestershire Archaeological Society*, vol. 102 (1984), pp. 76–81; *Victoria County History of Gloucestershire*, vol. IV, pp. 245–7 (the latter cites *DB*'s figure of 16 houses destroyed for the castle-site but not the more probable 24 of Evesham K).

4. British Library, Cotton MS. Vespasian XXV, fols. 57r–62r: the description of Gloucester is on fol. 57r. The text is translated in J. S. Moore, ed, *Domesday Book: Gloucestershire* (Chichester, 1982), Appendix.

5. *Victoria County History of Gloucestershire*, vol. IV, pp. 2, 5–9, 8, 10–11, 14, 18, 292, 295, 297, 300, 303, 308, 310, 386, 391.

6. The average household-size in Anglo-Norman England was of the order of 4.5 – 5.0 people (see above, pp. 19, 24, and references cited, nn. 40–1). But the average urban household was probably larger, since it would often include resident apprentices as well as servants.

7. H. C. Darby, I. B. Terrett, *Domesday Geography of Midland England* (Cambridge, 1954), p. 19; *Victoria County History of Gloucestershire*, vol. IV, p. 13.

8. Welsh raiding is reported in the Anglo-Saxon Chronicle in 1065 (C, D and E texts) and 1067 (D text): *ASC (DTW)*, pp. 137–8, 146; *ASC (G)*, pp. 190–1; *EHD*, vol. II, pp. 140–1, 151 (Page references to the Chronicle are given to the standard translation by D. Douglas, S. I. Whitelock, eds, *The Anglo-Saxon Chronicle* (London, 1961), [abbreviated as *ASC (DTW)*], reprinted in D. C. Douglas and D. W. Greenaway, ed, *English Historical Documents, vol.II* (London, 2nd edn, 1981), [abbreviated as *EHD*, vol.II] and to the well known translation by G.N. Garmonsway, ed, *The Anglo-Saxon Chronicle* (London, 2nd edn, 1972) [abbreviated as *ASC (G)*]. See also R. R. Davies, *Conquest, Co-existence and Change: Wales, 1063–1415* (Oxford, 1987), pt. I; L.H. Nelson, *The Normans in South Wales, 1070–1171* (Austin (USA), 1966), chaps. ii, v-vii; J. Meisel, *Barons of the Welsh Frontier: the Corbet, Pantulf and Fitz Warin families, 1066–1272* (Lincoln (USA), 1980), pt.III; F.C. Suppe, *Military Institutions on the Welsh Marches: Shropshire, A.D.1066–1300* (Woodbridge, 1994), chap. 1 and Appendix 1.

9. Winchcombe's burgess population is also given in Evesham K, on fol. 59r.

10. David Hill has tentatively suggested that a charter of Ethelred the Unready of 1007 granting land at Waltham St Lawrence (Berks) (P. H. Sawyer, *Anglo-Saxon Charters An annotated list and bibliography* (London, 1968), p. 280, no. 915) may have been drawn-up at Berkeley: '*Acta est huius donationis cartula in novo uidelicet oppido, quod regio vocatur Beorchore*' (D. H. Hill, 'Trends in the development of Towns during the reign of Ethelred II', in D. Hill, ed, 'Ethelred the Unready: Papers from the Millenary Conference' (*British Archaeological Reports, British Series*, vol. 59 (1978), p. 225).), a reference I owe to Michael Hare. But Margaret Gelling, *Early Charters of the Thames Valley* (Leicester, 1979), p.64, no.127, does not identify *Beorchore*, and Hill's identification has not been endorsed by any place-name scholar. Dr Ann Williams in conversation has confirmed that '*Beorchore*' cannot be a misreading of the known early forms for Berkeley (*Be(o)rclea*, 'birch clearing': A. H. Smith, ed, 'Place-Names of Gloucestershire, pt. 2' (*English Place-Names Society*, vol. XXXIX (1964), pp. 211–2)), but might represent an alternative name 'birch cliff' which the location of Berkeley on the eastern side of the Severn makes plausible. Nevertheless, the possession of a mint was a pre-eminent sign of borough-status in late Anglo-Saxon England (H. R. Loyn, 'Boroughs and Mints, AD 900–1066', in R. H. M. Dolley, ed, *Anglo-Saxon Coins* (London, 1961), pp. 122, 131–2; *idem*, 'Progress in Anglo-Saxon monetary history', in M.A.S. Blackburn, ed, *Anglo-Saxon Monetary History* (Leicester, 1986), pp. 6–7), and there was certainly a mint at Berkeley with two moneyers working in Edward the Confessor's reign (G.C. Brooke, *English Coins from the seventh century to the present day* (London, 3rd edn, 1950), p. 70; G. Galster, ed, *Sylloge of Coins of the British Isles*, vol. 18 (1972), pl. 28, nos. 748–9; L. V. Grinsell, C. E. Blunt, M. Dolley, eds, *Sylloge of Coins of the British Isles*, vol. 19 (1973), pl. IX, no. 193; A. Freeman, 'The Moneyer and the Mint under Edward the Confessor' (*British Archaeological Reports, British Series*, vol. 145 (1985), pt. 2, pp.380–2; J. J. North, *English Hammered Coinage, Volume I, Early Anglo-Saxon to Henry III , c.600–1272* (London, 3rd edn, 1994), pp. 182, 230–1 and plate 14, no.17).), though this ceased to operate after the Norman Conquest (E. J. Harris, 'The Moneyers of the Norman Kings and the types they are known to have struck' (*Seaby Coin and Medal Bulletin*, no. 774 (1983), p. 34).). Given the existence of the mint on a royal manor in the Confessor's reign, Berkeley certainly ranked as a borough before 1066, and the failure of *DB* to record its burghal status in 1086 may relate to the loss of its mint after 1066. Whether it was a borough before 1042 must for the present remain an open question.

11. See references cited in J. S. Moore, '"Quot homines?" The population of Domesday England' (*Anglo-Norman Studies*, vol. 19 (1997), p. 326, n. 58).

12. H. P. R. Finberg, M. W. Beresford, *English Medieval Boroughs. A Hand-list* (Newton Abbot, 1973), esp. pp. 37–40.

13. J. S. Moore, 'The Sudeley and Toddington Area in Domesday Book', in Lord Sudeley, ed, *The Sudeleys – Lords of Toddington* (London, 1987), p. 69, map. 3.

14. Anglo-Saxon Chronicle, 1085 (E text) 1085: *ASC (DWT)*, pp. 161–2; *ASC (G)*, p. 216; *EHD*, vol. II, p. 168.

15. *DB*, vol. II, fol. 450a.

16. *EHD*, vol. II, p. 914. The statement that 'the King ordered that all should be written in one volume' is important because it could not have been derived from *DB* itself which, as we have seen, was in two volumes; it must have come from a quite independent source, perhaps either Wulfstan, bishop of Worcester, or his successor Samson who in 1086 was a royal clerk certainly involved in the Domesday survey.

17. D.R. Bates, ed, *Regesta Regum Anglo-Normannorum. The Acta of William I (1066–1087)* (Oxford, 1998), pp. 82, 741, after quoting the Anglo-Saxon Chronicle as evidence for William crossing from the Isle of Wight to Normandy sometime after 1 August, states that when in Normandy he confirmed a diploma for St-Amand of Rouen (no. 242) late in 1086 or in 1087.

18. Anglo-Saxon Chronicle, 1086 (E text): *SC (DWT)*, p. 162; *ASC (G)*, p. 217; *EHD*, vol.II, p. 168.

19. W.H. Stevenson, 'A Contemporary Description of the Domesday Survey' (*English Historical Review*, vol. 22 (1907), pp. 72–84); translation in *EHD*, vol. II, p. 912.

20. B. Thorpe, ed, *Florence of Worcester, Chronicon ex Chronicis* (London, 2 vols, 1848), vol. II, p. 18, translated in *EHD*, vol. II, p. 914; see now P. McGurk, ed, *The Chronicle of John of Worcester, vol. III, 1067–1140* (Oxford, 1998), pp. 44–5. A full account of the development of the text and its sources must await Dr McGurk's Introduction in Vol.I, but my remarks are based on P. McGurk, R. R. Darlington, eds, *The Chronicle of John of Worcester, vol. II, 450–1066* (Oxford, 1995), pp. xvii-iii, xxi, lix, lxvii–xxiv, lxxix–xxxi.

21. D. Greenway, ed, *Henry of Huntingdon, Historia Anglorum. The History of the English People* (Oxford, 1996), pp. 400–1. As we have seen, *DB* is not a good record of castles, mentioning about one in ten (see above, p. 24, and reference cited, n. 50). The statement that the 'original returns' were still preserved at Winchester in the 1130s is important; they presumably disappeared when Winchester was burnt during the siege of 1144.

22. C. Johnson, ed, *Richard Fitz Nigel, Dialogus de Scaccario. The Course of the Exchequer* (Oxford, 2nd edn, 1983), p. 63.

23. The following account is based on V. H. Galbraith, *The Making of Domesday Book* (Oxford, 1961), which radically revised the then standard version based on J. H. Round, *Feudal England* (London, 1895), pp. 3–146, and F. W. Maitland, *Domesday Book and Beyond* (Cambridge, 1897), pp. 1–25. Since Galbraith wrote in strong reaction against the views of Round in particular, his own views have been modified by subsequent work which has re-emphasized the importance of oral evidence given by hundred juries in county courts.

24. Moore, '"Quot homines?" The population of Domesday England', p. 315.

25. The identification of the 'man behind Domesday' as William of Saint-Calais is due to P. Chaplais, 'William of Saint-Calais and the Domesday Survey', in J. C. Holt, ed, *Domesday Studies* (Woodbridge, 1987), pp. 65–77.

26. C. P. Lewis, 'The Earldom of Surrey and the Date of Domesday Book' (*Historical Research*, vol. 63 (1990), pp. 329–36) and D. Bates, 'Two Ramsey Abbey writs and the Domesday Survey' (*Historical Research*, vol. 63 (1990), pp. 337–9) together demonstrated that work on *DB* was still in progress in 1088.

27. N. E. S. A. Hamilton, ed, *Inquisitio Cantabrigiensis* (London, 1876), p. 97, translated in *EHD*, II, p. 946.

28. Anglo-Saxon Chronicle, 1085 (E text): *ASC (DWT)*, p. 161; *ASC (G)*, pp. 215–6; *EHD*, vol. II, p. 167.

29. For the element of illegal expropriation after 1066 see R. Fleming, *Kings and Lords in Conquest England* (Cambridge, 1991), pt. II. For the increasing contemporary stress on security of tenure and the inheritability of land, see J. Hudson, *Land, Law and Lordship in Anglo-Norman England* (Oxford, 1994), pts. I–II.

30. J. Holt, '1086', in Holt, ed, *Domesday Studies*, pp. 41–64.

31. C. S. Taylor, *An Analysis of the Gloucestershire Domesday* (Bristol, 1889), pp. 16, 19.

32. G. D. Snooks in R. H. Britnell, B. M. S. Campbell, eds, *A Commercialising Economy: England, 1085 to c.1300* (Manchester, 1995), p. 28; *cp* p. 31. It is the totality implied in the words 'comprehensive and reliable' that I cannot accept; I accept that *DB* was *generally* complete and reliable.

33. The hypotheses of the 'five-hide' and 'six-carucate' units were first put forward by Round, *Feudal England*, pp. 69–82, 87–90. For a recent restatement, see R. A. Leaver, 'Five hides in ten counties' (*Economic History Review*, 2nd ser, vol. 41 (1988), pp. 525–42).

34. M.M. Chibnall, ed, *Charters and Custumals of the Abbey of Holy Trinity, Caen* (Oxford, 1982), p. 37, n. 6.

35. Moore, '"Quot homines?" The population of Domesday England', pp. 315–9.

36. H. M. Taylor, J. Taylor, *Anglo-Saxon Architecture* (Cambridge, 3 vols, 1965–78); for Pucklechurch, a name recorded in Anglo-Saxon charters as well as in *DB*, see A. H. Smith, 'The Place-Names of Gloucestershire', pt. iii (*English Place-Names Society*, vol. XL (1964), pp. 64–5). For Deerhurst see now P. Wormald, *How do we know so much about Anglo-Saxon Deerhurst?* (Deerhurst, 1993), and C. Heighway, *Deerhurst St Mary and Gloucester St Oswald: Two Saxon Minsters* (Deerhurst, 1994), and for Odda, A. Williams, *Land, power and politics: the family and career of Odda of Deerhurst* (Deerhurst, 1997).

37. To elaborate on an important point raised in questions after this lecture, the *DB* 'villager' (*villanus*) was still personally a free man with access to the royal courts (L. J. Downer, ed, *Leges Henrici Primi* (Oxford, 1972)); the later 'villein' was not free in status and was consequently denied access to the royal courts (P. Vinogradoff, *Villainage in England* (Oxford, 1892), chaps. I–V; Vinogradoff, *English Society in the Eleventh Century* (Oxford, 1908), pp.219–470), though both held their land by a dependant tenure from their manorial lords (P.R. Hyams, *King, Lords and Peasants in Medieval England. The Common Law of Villeinage in the Twelfth and Thirteenth Centuries* (Oxford, 1980)). The *DB* slave was legally a chattel, the personal property of his owner (J. S. Moore, 'Domesday Slavery' (*Anglo-Norman Studies*, vol. 11 (1989), pp. 191–2, 212–3)); the 'serf', though unfree in status (so that 'villein' and 'serf' are synonymous terms by the thirteenth century), was not without civil rights, and was recognised in the thirteenth century by the Crown as being able to own moveable property (chattels) which did not belong to his lord and which was taxed by the Crown from 1225 onwards. The confusion arose because the Latin words *villanus* and *servus* remained in use from the eleventh century onwards but the meaning of both changed with the development of personal serfdom and villeinage tenure after *c.*1180.

38. Hamilton, ed, *Inquisitio Cantabrigiensis*, p.97, translated in *EHD*, vol.II, p.946.

39. Moore, 'Domesday Slavery', pp. 216–9.

40. P. Laslett, *Household and Family in Past Time* (Cambridge, 1972), chaps.1, 4–5.

41. J. T. Krause, 'The Medieval Household: Large or Small?' (*Economic History Review*, 2nd ser, vol. 9 (1957), pp. 420–32); H. E. Hallam, 'Some Thirteenth-Century Censuses' (*Economic History Review*, 2nd ser, vol. 10 (1958), pp. 340–61); J. S. Moore, 'The Anglo-Norman Family: Size and Structure' (*Anglo-Norman Studies*, vol. 14 (1992), pp. 153–96).

42. G. Orwell, *Nineteen Eighty-Four* (London, 1949), pp. 189, 206–7.

43. M.M. Postan, 'The Chronology of Labour Services' (*Transactions of the Royal Historical Society*, 4th ser, vol. 20 (1937), pp. 169–93), repr. with revisions in M. M. Postan, *Essays on Medieval Agriculture and General Problems of the Medieval Economy* (Cambridge, 1973), pp. 89–106; R. Lennard, *Rural England, 1086–1135* (Oxford, 1959), chaps.V–VII.

44. Chibnall, ed, *Charters and Custumals of the Abbey of Holy Trinity, Caen*, pp.34–7.

45. D. Royce, ed, *Landboc sive Registrum Monasterii de Winchelcumba* (Exeter, 2 vols, 1892, 1903), vol. I, pp. 219–25. I hope to print this survey with a full analysis elsewhere.

46. For the decline of slavery, see Moore, 'Domesday Slavery', pp. 219–20, and D. A. E. Pelteret, *Slavery in Early Medieval England from the reign of Alfred until the Twelfth Century* (Woodbridge, 1995), pp. 251–9. It is wrong to say that the slaves joined the villagers and therefore contributed to their decline into serfdom in the later twelfth and thirteenth centuries (A. L. Poole, *Obligations of Society in the XII and XIII Centuries* (Oxford, 1946), p.12). Poole later correctly stated that freed slaves 'joined ... the bordars and cottagers' *(From Domesday Book to Magna Carta, 1087–1216* (Oxford, 2nd edn, 1955), p. 40).

47. Moore, 'Domesday Slavery', pp. 203–7; R. H. Britnell, *The commercialisation of English society, 1000–1500* (Cambridge, 1993), chaps. 1–2; Britnell and Campbell, eds, *A Commercialising Economy: England, 1085 to c.1300*, chaps. 1–3.

48. Moore, 'The Anglo-Norman Family: Size and Structure'.

49. Moore, '"Quot homines?"' The population of Domesday England', pp. 322–3, 326–7.

50. R. Eales, 'Royal Power and Castles in Norman England', in C. Harper-Bill and R. Harvey, ed, *The Ideals and Practice of Medieval Knighthood*, vol. III (1990), pp. 54–63). For those castles mentioned in *DB*, see C.G. Harfield, 'A Hand-List of Castles recorded in the Domesday Book' *(English Historical Review*, vol. 106 (1991), pp. 371–92).

51. Moore, '"Quot homines?"' The population of Domesday England', p. 334.

52. D. Hooke, *The Anglo-Saxon Landscape of North Gloucestershire* (Deerhurst, 1993).

53. The authoritative study of place- and field-names in N. Gloucestershire is Smith, 'The Place-Names of Gloucestershire' pt. ii. But my own detailed work in S. Gloucestershire suggests that Smith's collection of field-names was often cursory and could now be considerably expanded.

54. Two excellent guides are B. P. Hindle, *Maps for Local History* (London, 1988) and D. Smith, *Maps and Plans for the local historian and collector* (London, 1988).

55. See, for a good introduction, N. W. Alcock, *Old Title Deeds. A guide for local and family historians* (Chichester, 1986).

56. C. Ross, M. Devine, eds, *The Cartulary of Cirencester Abbey* (Oxford, 3 vols, 1964, 1971). The unprinted Llanthony cartularies are PRO C 115/A.1–2, 4–6, 8–9. Details of other cartularies will be found in the now outdated G. R. C. Davis, *Medieval Cartularies of Great Britain* (London, 1958).

57. For an example from N.E. Gloucestershire, see Moore, 'The Sudeley and Toddington Area in Domesday Book', pp.54–8.

58. See C. Clark, '*Willelmus Rex? vel alius Willelmus*' (*Nomina*, vol.11 (1987), pp.7–33), repr. in P. Jackson, ed, *Words, Names and History* (Woodbridge, 1995), pp.280–98).

59. A. Williams, *The English and the Norman Conquest* (Woodbridge, 1995).

60. The local picture, with detailed references to the national literature, is excellently presented by S. Bassett, *The origin of the parishes of the Deerhurst area* (Deerhurst, 1998).

61. I am most grateful to Michael Hare for his invitation to deliver the 1998 Deerhurst Lecture and for his subsequent help in preparing this paper for publication, to Mrs Sue Grice (Department of Archaeology, University of Bristol) for drawing the maps, to Mrs Susan Campbell and her daughter Louise for distributing handouts at the lecture, and to the Friends of Deerhurst for their hospitality after the lecture and for agreeing to publish the lecture. My wife and children know well how much I rely on their love and support.

APPENDIX:
DOMESDAY BOOK ENTRIES AND DERIVED DATA, NORTH – CENTRAL GLOUCESTERSHIRE

Folio	Chap	Entry	Manor	Landholder 1066
Cheltenham Hundred:				
162d	1	1	Cheltenham	King Edward
162d	1	1	Cheltenham (Glebe)	Reinbald
164c	2	5	Swindon	Archbishop Stigand
165a	4	1	Prestbury	Bishop of Hereford
167c	38	1	Broadwell in Leckhampton	Osgot
170c	78	9	Leckhampton	Beorhtric, Orderic
Deerhurst Hundred:				
166b	19	1	Deerhurst	Westminster Abbey
166b	19	2	Hardwicke, Bourton on the Hill, Todenham, Sutton under Brailes.	Westminster Abbey
			Elmstone, Ellings, Wightfield, Todenham, Hayden, Rye, Oridge.	? 10 Riding men from Westminster Abbey
166b	20	1	Uckington, Staverton, Coln, St Dennis, Calcot, etc	St Denis', Paris
			Woolstone, Leigh, Deerhurst Walton, etc	St Denis', Paris
Dudstone Hundred:				
162d	1	2	King's Barton	King Edward
162d	1	2	Matson	King Edward
162d	1	2	Brawn	Wigot from
169c	64	1		Archbishop Ældred
162d	1	2	Upton St Leonards	Pagan from
170b	70	1		Alwine the sheriff
162d	1	2	Murrells End	Alwine the sheriff
162d	1	3	Haresfield, Down Hatherley, Sandhurst	Edmer, thegn
162d	1	4	Harescombe	Wiflet
162d	1	5	Brookthorpe	AElfric
162d	1	6	Netheridge in Quedgeley	Wulfward
164b	1	62	Hempsted	Edric Lang
164c	2	1	Churchdown	Archbishop Stigand
164c	2	2	Hucclecote	Archbishop Stigand
164c	2	3	Bishop's Norton	Archbishop Stigand
165c	10	1	Abbots Barton, Barnwood, Tuffley, Morwents End	St Peter's, Gloucester
167a	31	11	Badgeworth	Alfstan
167c	36	1	Wotton	Godric
168d	53	6	Whaddon	5 brothers
169b	63	1	Brockworth	Thorkell
170c	78	6	Elmore	? Edward

Landholder (1086)	Sub-Tenant (1086)	Hidage		Demesne ploughs
		H	V	
King William	King's reeve	8	2	4
Reinbald	'priests'	1	2	2
St Oswald's, Gloucester	Archbishop Thomas	3	0	2
Bishop of Hereford		10	0	3
William Leofric		3	0	2
King William	Beorhtric	4	0	1
Westminster Abbey		5	0	3
Westminster Abbey		25	0	13
Westminster Abbey	7 knights; Abbot Baldwin	18	0	11.5
St Denis', Paris		50	0	15
St Denis', Paris		7	2	5
King William	King's reeve	9	0	4
King William	2 free men	2	0	0
King William	Miles Crispin		3	1
King William	Humphrey of Maidenhill	1	0	1
King William	Nigel the doctor		3	0
King William		2	0	8
King William	Wiflet		3	2
King William			3	2
King William	Avenel the cook		2	2
King William		5	0	3
Archbishop Thomas		15	2	2
Archbishop Thomas		4	0	2
Archbishop Thomas	Walkelin	5	2	2
St Peter's, Gloucester		21	3	9
William of Eu		8	0	6
William Breakwolf		2	0	2
Durand of Gloucester		5	0	5
Hugh Donkey		5	0	2
King William	Edward		2	1

Manor	Free Men	Villagers	Small-holders	Tenants' ploughs
Cheltenham Hundred:				
Cheltenham	0	24	12	18
Cheltenham (Glebe)	0	0	0	0
Swindon	0	7	2	7
Prestbury	0	18	5	9
	2	0	0	2
Broadwell in Leckhampton	0	2	8	1
Leckhampton	0	0	9	3
Deerhurst Hundred:				
Deerhurst	0	20	8	10
Hardwicke, Bourton on the Hill, Todenham,				
Sutton under Brailes	0	45	27	21
Elmstone, Ellings, Wightfield, Todenham,				
Hayden, Rye, Oridge, etc	0	14	27	7
Uckington, Staverton, Coln St Dennis,				
Calcot, etc	5	75	12	39
Woolstone, Leigh, Deerhurst Walton, etc	1	5	18	9
Dudstone Hundred:				
King's Barton	0	14	18	9
Matson	2	0	0	9
Brawn	0	0	7	2
Upton St Leonards	0	0	4	2
Murrells End	0	0	0	0
Haresfield, Down Hatherley, Sandhurst	0	4	4	5
Harescombe	0	0	2	0
Brookthorpe	0	1	3	0
Netheridge in Quedgeley	0	0	0	0
Hempsted	0	6	8	6
Churchdown	7	18	5	30
Hucclecote	0	11	5	11
Bishop's Norton	0	15	0	15
Abbots Barton, Barnwood, Tuffley,				
Morwents End	0	42	21	45
Badgeworth	0	20	14	24
Wotton	0	0	4	0
Whaddon	0	11	7	5
Brockworth	4	8	6	15
Elmore	0	0	6	2

Slaves	Mills	Meadow (acres)	Woodland	Value 1066 (£)	Value 1086 (£)	Change in value, 1066–86 (%)
7 } 0	5	N/A	N/A	N/A	N/A	N/A
4	N/A	N/A	N/A	3	4.5	50
11 0	N/A	20	1L × 0.5L }	12	16	33.3
4	N/A	N/A	1F × 1F	2	2	0
3	N/A	N/A	2F × 2F	N/A	1.5	N/A
6	N/A	60	2L × 0.5L	10	10	0
37	4	20	1L × 0.5L	41	40	-2.4
14	N/A	20	N/A			
38	4	36	2.5L × 1.25L }	26.5	30	13.2
N/A	N/A	38	0.5L × 2F			
7	3	N/A	N/A	N/A	N/A	N/A
N/A	N/A	N/A	N/A	N/A	N/A	N/A
N/A	N/A	N/A	N/A	2	1.5	−25
3	N/A	N/A	N/A	1.5	1	−33.3
0	N/A	N/A	N/A	N/A	N/A	N/A
30	N/A	N/A	N/A	N/A }		
5	N/A	N/A	N/A	N/A }	46.6	N/A
4	N/A	N/A	N/A	N/A		
4	N/A	N/A	N/A	N/A	N/A	N/A
6	N/A	N/A	N/A	N/A	3	N/A
N/A	N/A	N/A	0.5L × 3F	13	12	−7.7
N/A	1	N/A	1L × 0.5L	4	4	0
4	1	N/A	N/A	4	4	0
12	1	120	5L × 3L	8	24	200
17	1	N/A	2L × 1L	15	13	−13.3
4	N/A	N/A	N/A	1.5	3	100
N/A	N/A	N/A	N/A	8	5	−37.5
4	1	N/A	1L × 0.5L	6	5	−16.7
N/A	N/A	N/A	N/A	N/A	1.5	N/A

Manor	Demesne ploughs/ All ploughs (%)	Average		Estimated population	Resident Lord
		tenant holding (ploughs)	tenant holding (virgates)		
Cheltenham Hundred:					
Cheltenham	17	0.7	3	205	N
Cheltenham (Glebe)	100	N/A	N/A	50	N
Swindon	22	1	4	60	N
Prestbury	21	0.5	2	160	N
		1	4	10	N
Broadwell in Leckhampton	66	0.5	2	70	N
Leckhampton	25	0.3	1	70	Y
Deerhurst Hundred:					
Deerhurst	23	0.5	2	160	N
Hardwicke, Bourton on the Hill, Todenham, Sutton under Brailes	38	0.5	2	520	N
Elmstone, Ellings, Wightfield, Todenham, Hayden, Rye, Oridge, etc	62	0.5	2	260	N
Uckington, Staverton, Coln St Dennis, Calcot, etc	28	0.5	2	620	N
Woolstone, Leigh, Deerhurst Walton, etc	36	1	4	115	N
King's Barton	18	0.5	2	190	N
Matson	0	4.5	18	10	Y
Brawn	33	0.3	1	30	N
Upton St Leonards	33	0.5	2	40	Y
Murrells End					N
Haresfield, Down Hatherley, Sandhurst	62	1	4	180	N
Harescombe	100			40	Y
Brookthorpe			100	40	N
Netheridge in Quedgeley	100			30	Y
Hempsted	33	0.8	3	100	N
Churchdown	6	1.2	5	140	N
Hucclecote	15	1	4	80	N
Bishop's Norton	12	1	4	100	Y
Abbots Barton, Barnwood, Tuffley, Morwents End	17	1	4	360	N
Badgeworth	20	1	4	240	N
Wotton	100			50	Y
Whaddon	50	0.5	2	90	N
Brockworth	12	1	4	100	N
Elmore	33	0.33	1	40	Y

Other information

4 villagers, 2 smallholders, 3 mills, 1 demesne plough added since 1066; values in both 1066 and 1086 include unpriced items.
Assumed 10–12 canons.

Value includes outlier of Sevenhampton; also 1 burgess in Winchcombe.
Free men = 1 priest, 1 riding man.
William Leofric's main manor was probably Hailes.
Beorhtric probably a resident lord.

Also 'water-meadows 3F x 1F'.

Also '8 sesters of honey' rendered in 1066.

Also 30 burgesses in Gloucester, 2 burgesses in Winchcombe.

8 smallholders, 2 mills, 1 demesne plough added since 1066; values in both 1066 and 1086 include unpriced items.

'3 men' in first entry probably in error for 7 smallholders; also half a fishery.
'4 men' in first entry = 4 smallholders in second entry;
Humphrey probably resident lord; meadows only at Sezincote.
No other details given.

Meadow 'sufficient for the ploughs'.
Meadow 'for the ploughs'; Wiflet probably resident lord.

Also 'half a fishery'.
Free men = Riding men.

Walkelin possibly a resident lord.

William Breakwolf probably resident lord.
'1 villager' probably a mistake for 11 villagers.
Free men = 1 priest, 2 freemen, 1 reeve.
Edward probably resident lord.

Folio	Chap	Entry	Manor	Landholder 1066

Greston Hundred:

165d	11	3	Twyning	Winchcombe Abbey

Tewkesbury Hundred:

163b	1	24	Tewkesbury	Beorhtric son of Ælfgar
163b	1	24	Southwick, Tredington, Fiddington, Pamington, Natton, Walton Cardiff, Aston on Carrant	Beorhtric son of Ælfgar
163c	1	24	Aston on Carrant	1 Riding Man
			Walton Cardiff	1 Riding Man
			Fiddington	1 Riding Man
163c	1	25	Oxenton	Beorhtric son of Ælfgar
163c	1	30	Great Washbourne	Tewkesbury Church
163c	1	31–2	Fiddington, Natton	Tewkesbury Church
163c	1	33	Stanley Pontlarge	Tewkesbury Church
163c	1	35	Forthampton	Beorhtric son of Ælfgar
163d	1	43	Alderton, Dixton, Hentage	Dunning
163d	1	44	Mythe in Twyning	Beorhtric son of Ælfgar
163d	1	45	Stoke Orchard	Hermer, Alwine

Tibblestone Hundred:

165a	3	7	Bishops Cleeve	Bishop of Worcester
			Southam, Sapperton, Gotherington	Bishop of Worcester

TOTALS:

Abbreviations: F = Furlong. H = Hides. L = League. V = Virgates (Yardlands).

Note:
All percentages and derived figures have been rounded to the first decimal place. Estimated populations have also been rounded (see text).

Landholder (1086)	Sub-Tenant (1086)	Hidage		Demesne ploughs
		H	V	
Winchcombe Abbey		3	0	2
King William		45	0	13
King William		35	2	0
King William	Gerard	6	0	10
King William	Ralph	3	0	
King William	Bernard	2	0	
King William		5	0	5
King William	Tewkesbury Church	3	0	2
King William	Tewkesbury Church	3	0	1
King William	Tewkesbury Church	4	2	1
King William		9	0	2
King William	Humphrey	12	0	4
King William	John the Chamberlain	2	2	4
King William	Bernard	2	3	1
Bishop of Worcester		14	0	3
Bishop of Worcester	Durand of Gloucester, Ralph, Thurstan son of Rolf	16	0	8
		391	2	171.5

Manor	Free Men	Villagers	Small-holders	Tenants' ploughs
Greston Hundred:				
Twyning	0	24	8	27
Tewkesbury Hundred:				
Tewkesbury	13	0	16	0
Southwick, Tredington, Fiddington,				
Pamington, Natton, Walton Cardiff,	9	21	0	26
Aston on Carrant		5	1	1
Aston on Carrant				
Walton Cardiff	0	4	1	1
Fiddington				
Oxenton	2	5	0	7
Great Washbourne	0	6	1	3
Fiddington, Natton	0	3	0	2
Stanley Pontlarge	0	4	3	2
Forthampton	0	20	0	0
Alderton, Dixton, Hentage	0	5	8	3
	1	0	0	1
Mythe in Twyning	0	0	0	0
Stoke Orchard	0	0	0	0
Tibblestone Hundred:				
Bishops Cleeve	0	16	19	16
	1	0	0	2
	1	0	0	2
Southam, Sapperton, Gotherington	0	22	7	13
TOTALS:	48	495	306	416
TOTALS (ADJUSTED):				

Slaves	Mills	Meadow (acres)	Woodland	Value 1066 (£)	Value 1086 (£)	Change in value, 1066–86 (%)
10		40	2F × 1F	8	7	−12.5
72	2 ⎫					
		120	1.5L × 1.5L	100	50	−50
0						
9	1 ⎭					
0		18		10	10	0
12		24		8	8	0
10				3	3	0
				1	1	0
5				4	2	−50
6				10	8	−20
	⎬	12		11	6	−45.5
		3		2	2	0
		4		3	2	−33.3
8			⎫			
			⎬	36	26	−27.8
20	1		⎭			
376	24	535		1419.5	1438.7	1.4
				1406.5	1373.5	−2.3

Manor	Demesne ploughs/ All ploughs (%)	Average tenant holding (ploughs)	tenant holding (virgates)	Estimated population	Resident Lord
Greston Hundred:					
Twyning	7	1	4	200	N
Tewkesbury Hundred:					
Tewkesbury	⎫			480	N
Southwick, Tredington, Fiddington, Pamington, Natton, Walton Cardiff, Aston on Carrant	⎬ 29	1	4	140	N
Aston on Carrant	⎭			30	N
Walton Cardiff	91	0.3	1	80	Y
Fiddington					N
Oxenton	42	1	4	90	N
Great Washbourne	40	0.5	2	80	N
Fiddington, Natton	66	0.7	3	15	N
Stanley Pontlarge	33	0.5	2	60	N
Forthampton	100			120	N
Alderton, Dixton, Hentage	50	0.5	2	60	N
		1	4	5	N
Mythe in Twyning	100				N
Stoke Orchard	100			10	Y
Tibblestone Hundred:					
Bishops Cleeve		1	4	200	N
		2	8	5	
	13	2	8	5	
Southam, Sapperton, Gotherington	38	0.5	2	230	N
TOTALS:				5970	
AVERAGES:	42	0.9	3.5	120	

Free men = burgesses; 1 demesne plough added since 1066; also 'a market which the queen set-up', 1 fishery and 'a salt-pan at Droitwich'; 50 slaves in 1066; 8 burgesses in Gloucester.

Free men = Riding men; villagers = freedmen.

Gerard's main manor was Kemerton.
Ralph was a resident lord.
Bernard's main manor was Stoke Orchard.
Free men = Riding men. Also 3 burgesses at Winchcombe.

3 villagers include 2 freedmen.

'Woodland'; 20 'villagers and smallholders'.
A burgess in Winchcombe.
Free man = Riding man.
John the Chamberlain's main manor was in Fairford.
Bernard probably a resident lord.

'A very small wood'; also '1 draught animal'.
Free man = Priest.
Free man = Riding man.
'some meadow'; also '3 draught animals'.

Manors with values stated in both 1066 and 1086: total fall 2.3%.

The Friends of Deerhurst Church
List of publications in print (August 2000)

Liturgy and Architecture in the Middle Ages by David Parsons
(Deerhurst Lecture 1986) £1.50

Deerhurst St Mary and Gloucester St Oswald: Two Saxon Minsters by
Carolyn Heighway (abbreviated text of the 1989 Deerhurst Lecture) £0.50

The Anglo-Saxon Landscape of North Gloucestershire by Della Hooke
(Deerhurst Lecture 1990) £1.25

How do we know so much about Anglo-Saxon Deerhurst? by Patrick
Wormald (Deerhurst Lecture 1991) £2.50

The two Anglo-Saxon minsters of Gloucester by Michael Hare (Deerhurst
Lecture 1992) £2.50

Land, power and politics: the family and career of Odda of Deerhurst
by Ann Williams (Deerhurst Lecture 1996) £2.00

The origins of the parishes of the Deerhurst area by Steven Bassett
(Deerhurst Lecture 1997) £2.50

*From Anglo-Saxon to Anglo-Norman: North Gloucestershire in Domesday
Book* by John Moore (Deerhurst Lecture 1998) £3.00

The Priory Church of St Mary at Deerhurst by Arnold Porter
(Guidebook, lavishly illustrated) £1.50

Publications may be obtained from The Secretary, The Friends of
Deerhurst Church, Daffodil Cottage, Deerhurst, Gloucester GL19 4BX.
Please add 35p for each publication for postage and packing.